DIFFERENT STEPS TO EFFECTIVE READING

JOHNSON LAWRENCE

DIFFERENT STEPS TO EFFECTIVE READING

(A Step by Step Guide)

DEDICATION

This book is dedicated to God Almighty

PREFACE

Different steps to effective reading is designed to make reading easy and interesting.

This book though systematic and self explanatory, is actually an aid to make teaching, spelling and reading easy and effective.

It is written with the mindset to help people no matter their level of reading to understand gradually how to read in a simple way.

This book begins reading right from the scratch to a good level, adding some grammatical terms, some moral and economic topics to help smoothen the spoken English of the reader or learner. TO GOD BE THE GLORY

TABLE OF CONTENTS

STEP ONE

LOWER CASE a-z

a b c d e f g h i j k l

m n o p q r s t u v w x

y z

STEP TWO: UPPER CASE LETTER A-Z

A B C D E F G H I J K L M

N O P Q R S T U V W X Y Z

SOUND /a/- /z/

/a/ /b/ /c/ /d/ /e/ /f/ /g/ /h/ /i/ /j/

/k/ /l/ /m/ /n/ /o/ /p/ /q/ /r/ /s/ /t/

/u/ /v/ /w/ /x/ /y/ /z/

STEP THREE: BLENDING OF LETTERS WITH OBJECTS

A

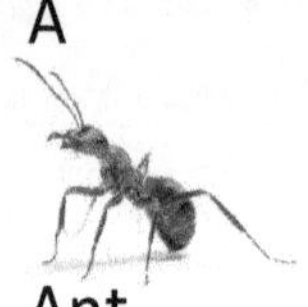

Ant

B

Ball

C

Cat

D

Dog

E

Egg

F

Fish

G

Girl

H

Hat

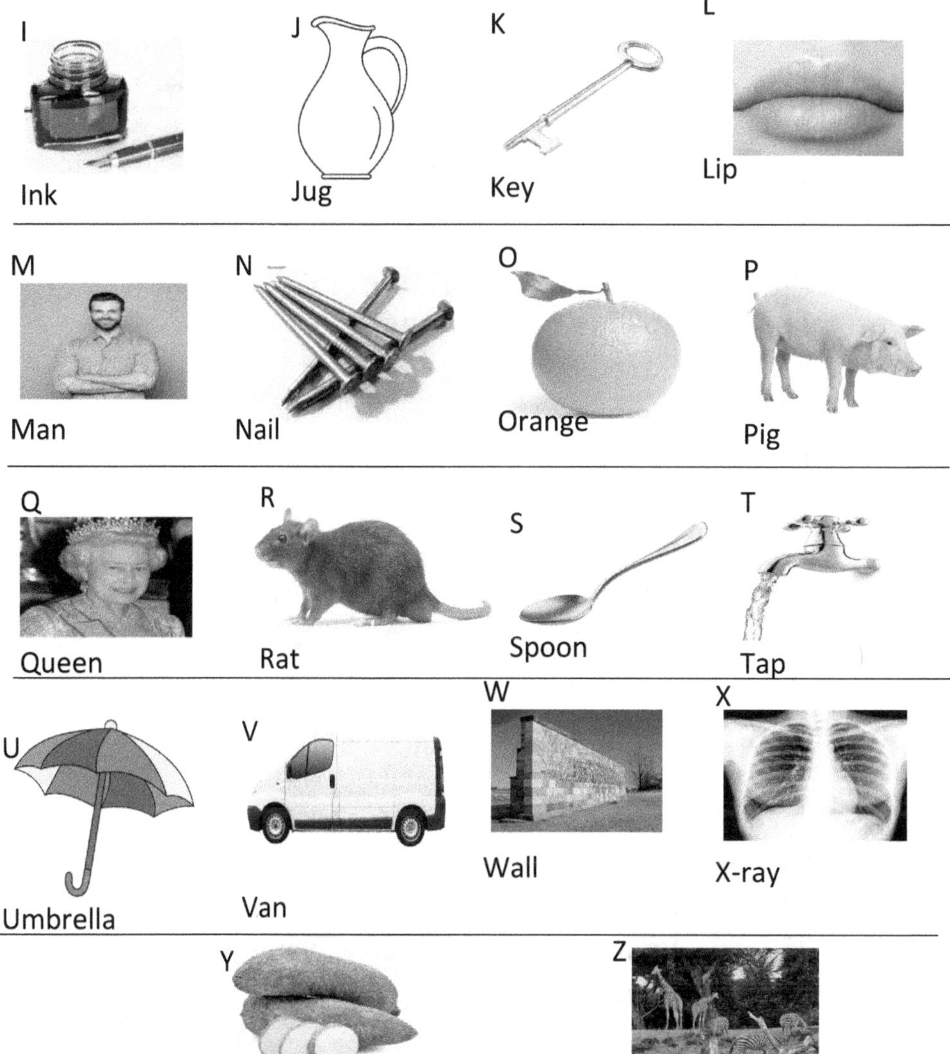
I
Ink
J
Jug
K
Key
L
Lip
M
Man
N
Nail
O
Orange
P
Pig
Q
Queen
R
Rat
S
Spoon
T
Tap
U
Umbrella
V
Van
W
Wall
X
X-ray
Y
Yam
Z
Zoo

SOUND AND WORDS

1.	Sound a	as	in	ant
2.	Sound b	as	in	ball
3.	Sound c	as	in	cat
4.	Sound d	as	in	dog
5.	Sound e	as	in	egg
6.	Sound f	as	in	fish
7.	Sound g	as	in	girl
8.	Sound h	as	in	hat
9.	Sound i	as	in	ink
10.	Sound j	as	in	jug
11.	Sound k	as	in	key
12.	Sound l	as	in	lip
13.	Sound m	as	in	man
14.	Sound n	as	in	nail
15.	Sound o	as	in	orange
16.	Sound p	as	in	pig
17.	Sound q	as	in	queen
18.	Sound r	as	in	rat
19.	Sound s	as	in	spoon
20.	Sound t	as	in	tap
21.	Sound u	as	in	umbrella
22.	Sound v	as	in	van
23.	Sound w	as	in	wall
24.	Sound x	as	in	x-ray
25.	Sound y	as	in	yam
26.	Sound z	as	in	zoo

STEP FOUR: Blending of 2 – letter words with vowel sound a, e, i, o, u

a + m = am

a + n =

a + t =

a – s =

i + t =

i + n =

i + s =

i + f =

o + f =

o + r =

o + n =

o + x =

u + p =

u + s =

Unblendable or Tricky words

be =	my =	lo =
he =	go =	to =
we =	do =	
me =	so =	
by =	no =	

FORMATION OF SENTENCES WITH TWO LETTER WORDS

1. He is on
2. He is in
3. We go up
4. Up we go
5. Do we go in
6. We go in
7. Is it on it?
8. It is on it
9. Is he by me?
10. He is by me

(STEP 5)

BLENDING OF 2 MEANINGLESS WORDS OR NON-CONVENTIONAL WORDS WITH VOWEL SOUND 'a'

b – a = ba

Take note that all the first letters are all consonant

1. b – a =
2. d – a =
3. g – a =
4. l – a =
5. n – a =
6. r – a =
7. t – a =
8. w – a =
9. z – a =
10. c – a =

11. f – a =
12. h – a =
13. m – a =
14. p – a =
15. s – a =
16. y – a =

(STEP 6)

BLENDING OF 3LETTER WORDS WITH VOWEL SOUND 'a'

b-a-t = bat

c-a-n =

d-a-d =

f-a-t =

g-a-p =

h-a-s =

l-a-p =

m-a-n =

p-a-t =

r-a-n =

t-a-p =

b-a-d =

c-a-t =

f-a-n =

g-a-s =

h-a-d =

m-a-t =

p-a-d =

r-a-t =

t-a-g =

STEP 7:

HAVEN'T GOTTEN USE TO THE 3 LETTER WORDS, LET'S MAKE SIMPLE SENTENCES WITH SOME OF THE WORDS.

1. The bat is on the tap
2. My bag is on the fan
3. The fat rat sat on a mat
4. My dad is a man
5. The man ran to the car.

STEP 8:

BLENDING OF TWO MEANINGLESS SOUNDS OR NON-COVENTIONAL WORDS WITH VOWEL SOUND "e"

1. B – e → Be
2. F – e →
3. M – e →
4. P – e →
5. S – e →
6. T – e →
7. Y – e →
8. D – e →
9. G – e →
10. L – e →

11. N – e ⟶

12. W – e ⟶ ☐

13. V – e ⟶ ☐

14. Z – e ⟶ ☐

STEP 9:

BLENDING OF 3 LETTER WORDS WITH VOWEL SOUND "e"

1. B – e – t =
2. F – e – d =
3. M – e – t =
4. M – e – n =
5. P – e – t =
6. S – e – t =
7. T – e – n =
8. Y – e – t =
9. G – e – t =
10. L – e – t =
11. N – e – t =
12. W – e – t =
13. V - e - t =
14. Z – e – d =

SIMPLE SENTENCES WITH 3 LETTER WORDS WITH VOWEL SOUND "e"

1. It is a jet
2. The net is on the bed
3. The pet is in the jet

4. It is a peg
5. Let ten men get the hen

STEP 10: BLENDING OF TWO MEANINGLESS SOUNDS OR NON-CONVENTIONAL WORDS WITH VOWEL SOUND 'I'

1. b – i = bi
2. d – i =
3. g – i =
4. l – i =
5. p – i =
6. w – i =
7. c – i =
8. f – i =
9. h – i =
10. m – i =
11. s – i =
12. z – i =

FORMATION OF 3-LETTER WORDS WITH VOWEL SOUND "i"

1. B – i – t = bit
2. D – i – g =
3. F – i – t =
4. H – i – s =
5. K – i – n =
6. L – i – p =
7. S – i – n =
8. W – i – g =
9. B – i – d =
10. D – i – d =
11. F – i – x =
12. H –i– t =
13. K- i - d =
14. L – i - d =

15. S – i - t =
16. W – i – n =

FORMATION OF SIMPLE SENTENCES WITH VOWEL SOUND 'i'

1. The kid is on the sit
2. Can I get the wig?
3. The wig is in the bin
4. I win the big pig
5. I sit on the bin

STEP 11: BLENDING OF TWO MEANINGLESS SOUNDS OR NON-CONVENTIONAL WORDS WITH VOWEL SOUND 'O'

1. B – o = Bo
2. D – o =
3. G – o =
4. L – o =
5. N – o =
6. R – o =
7. W – o =
8. Z – o =
9. C – o =
10. F – o =
11. H – o =
12. M – o =
13. P – o =
14. S – o =

BLENDING OF 3 – LETTER WORDS WITH VOWEL SOUND 'o'

1. B – o – x = Box
2. L – o – g =
3. M – o – p =

4. P – o – t =
5. C – o – t =
6. H- o – t =
7. N – o - n =
8. D – o – g =
9. D – o – t =
10. F- o - r =

FORMATION OF SIMPLE SENTENCES WITH VOWEL SOUND 'o'

1. The pot is on the mop.
2. The dog is on the log.
3. The pot is in the hut
4. It is a cot.
5. Non of the box is for me.

STEP 12: BLENDING OF TWO MEANINGLESS SOUNDS OR NON-CONVENTIONAL WORDS WITH VOWEL SOUND 'U'

1. B – u = Bu
2. G – u =
3. J – u =
4. L – u =
5. S – u =
6. M – u =
7. C – u =
8. F – u =
9. H – u =
10. R – u =

BLENDING OF 3 LETTER WORDS WITH VOWEL SOUND 'u'

1. B – u – t = But
2. C – u – t =
3. F – u – n =
4. H – u – t =

5. J – u – g =
6. M – u – d =
7. S – u – m =
8. R- u - n =
9. S – u - n =
10. G – u - m =

FORMATION OF SIMPLE SENTENCES WITH SOUND 'u'

1. It is a cup
2. The jug is in the sun
3. It is a rug
4. This is a mug
5. I run to the hut

HAVEN'T GOTTEN USE TO WORDS AND SENTENCES WITH VOWEL SOUND a,e,i,o,u

Read the following sentences formed with vowel sound a, e, i, o, u

1. The cat is on the bed
2. The fat man sat on the log
3. That dog sat on a mat
4. The sun is hot
5. The rat is wet
6. The pig is fat
7. She ran to the man
8. The jug is in the bin
9. He ran to his dad
10. The ball is on the tap

STEP 13

In this 13th step we'll be looking at words with Diagraph at the middle.

What is Diagraph: Diagraph is a combination of two letters that makes a single sound. Example: sound 'oa'

'<u>oa</u> ➡ as in :-

1. S-oa-p = Soap
2. C-oa-t =
3. G-oa-t =

4. R-oa-d =
5. F-oa-m =
6. L-oa-m =
7. G-oa-l =
8. B-oa-t =
9. T-oa-d =

FORMATION OF SENTENCES WITH SOUND 'oa'

1. The coat is in the boat
2. The soap is on the foam
3. It is a goat
4. The goal is on the road
5. It is a boat

STEP 14

Diagraph Sound 'ai'

'ai' as in :-

1. B-ai-l = Bail
2. F-ai-l =
3. G-ai-n =
4. H-ai-l =
5. J-ai-l =
6. L-ai-d =
7. M-ai-d =
8. N-ai-l =
9. P-ai-l =
10. R-ai-n =

FORMATION OF SENTENCES WITH SOUND 'ai'.

1. The maid is in the sail
2. I fail to nail the pail
3. It is a nail

4. I hail my God for my kids
5. The rain falls everyday

STEP 15

DIAGRAPH SOUND "ee"

"ee" as in:

1. B-ee = Bee
2. S-ee =
3. P-ee-l =
4. J-ee-p =
5. W-ee-k =
6. B-ee-f =
7. F-ee-l =
8. H-ee-l =
9. S-ee-n =
10. T-ee-n =
11. W-ee-l =
12. D-ee-p =
13. F-ee-d =
14. S-ee-d =
15. N-ee-d =
16. M-ee-t =
17. Fr-ee =
18. Gr-ee-n =
19. Sh-ee-p =

FORMATION OF SIMPLE SENTENCES WITH SOUND "ee"

1. I see the bee in the tree
2. The jeep has a tean weel
3. The week feel very deep
4. The seed is in the heel
5. The meat is in the beef

STEP16

DIAGRAPH SOUND "ay"

"ay" as in :

1. D-ay = Day
2. L-ay =
3. P-ay =
4. M-ay =
5. S-ay =
6. W-ay =
7. R-ay =
8. G-ay =
9. N-ay =
10. Pl-ay =
11. St-ay =
12. Cl-ay =
13. Pr-ay =
14. Tr-ay =
15. Spr-ay =

FORMATION OF SIMPLE SENTENCE WITH SOUND "ay"

1. Today's date is 12th may
2. She say the way she play
3. The tray is in the way
4. He stay to pray to God
5. I pay for the clay today

STEP 17

SOUND "ur"

"ur" as in :

1. T-ur-n = Turn
2. B-ur-n =
3. H-ur-t =
4. B-ur-nt =
5. B-ur-st =

6. C-ur-ve =
7. P-ur-se =
8. N-ur-se =
9. Ch-ur-ch =
10. P-ur-ple =

FORMATION OF SENTENCES WITH SOUND "ur"

1. I turn to see the queen
2. The nurse is in the church
3. He burnt all her cloths
4. The purple bag is big
5. They burst the ball in the goal

STEP 18

SOUND "ar"

1. St-ar = Star
2. C-ar =
3. M-ar-k =
4. F-ar =
5. H-ar-d =
6. H-ar-m =
7. C-ar-d =
8. B-ar-k =
9. D-ar-k =
10. F-ar-m =

FORMATION OF SENTENCES WITH SOUND "ar"

1. The big sky has a dark star
2. He park the car in the farm
3. She ran far to get the card
4. The dog bark in the dark
5. The red ball is hard

STEP 19

SOUND 'ou'

WORDS WITH SOUND 'ou'

1. Ou-t = out
2. L-ou-d =
3. P-ou-nd =
4. H-ou-se =
5. C-ou-nt =
6. S-ou-nd =
7. D-ou-bt =
8. M-ou-th =
9. r-ou-nd =
10. F-ou-nd =
11. C-ou-ch =
12. S-ou-th =
13. M-ou-se =
14. Pr-ou-d =
15. Sh-ou-t =
16. Sc-ou-t =
17. Bl-ou-se =
18. Cl-ou-d =

FORMATION OF SENTENCES WITH SOUND 'ou'

1. The boy's voice is too loud
2. The mouse is in the couch
3. She is proud of her house
4. The sound from her mouth is loud
5. Our house is around the south

STEP 20

SOUND ‘ow’

Words on sound ‘ow’

1. Ow-l = owl
2. C-ow =
3. N-ow =
4. H-ow =
5. B-ow =
6. F-ow-l =
7. T-ow-n =
8. G-ow-n =
9. Cr-ow-n =
10. Cr-ow-d =
11. Br-ow-n =
12. Dr-ow-n =
13. Fr-ow-n =
14. P-ow-n =
15. P-ow-der =

FORMATION OF SENTENCES WITH SOUND ‘OW’

1. The cow in the town is brown
2. She bow down to praise God
3. The fowl is in the crowd
4. There is fine flower on my gown
5. They crown the boy a king

STEP 21

SOUND ‘oy’

1. B-oy = Boy
2. T-oy =

3. J-oy =
4. R-oy =
5. En-j-oy =
6. Em-pl-oy =
7. Ann-oy =
8. Des-tr-oy =
9. B-oy-ish =
10. J-oy-ful =

FORMATION OF SENTENCES WITH SOUND 'oy"

1. I am full of joy
2. I have a toy
3. I enjoy eating rice and stew
4. The girl looks boyish
5. I was employed on Monday

STEP 22

SOUND 'al'

1. H-all = Hall
2. F-all =
3. B-all =
4. W-all =
5. C-all =
6. T-all =
7. T-al-k =
8. W-al-k =
9. Ch-al-k =
10. Sm-all =

FORMATION OF SENTENCES WITH SOUND 'al'

1. The ball is in the room
2. The boy fall into the pit
3. I have a small bag

4. She write with the chalk on the wall
5. My son is a tall boy

STEP 23

SOUND 'ea'

1. Ea-t = Eat
2. T-ea =
3. S-ea =
4. M-ea-t =
5. R-ea-d =
6. Ea-ch =
7. B-ea-t =
8. L-ea-f =
9. Ea-st =
10. H-ea-t =
11. M-ea-n =
12. R-ea-ch =
13. S-ea-t =
14. T-ea-m =
15. W-ea-k =
16. L-ea-k =
17. Cr-ea-m =
18. St-ea-m =
19. St-ea-l =
20. Ch-ea-p =
21. P-ea-ch =

FORMATION OF SENTENCE WITH SOUND 'ea'

1. The meat is in the sea
2. The cream is in the bread
3. I read my book everyday
4. I have a green leaf
5. The team are in the beach

STEP 24
WORDS WITH SOUND a-e (Sounds as letter 'A')

1. A-te = Ate
2. G-a-me =
3. L-a-ne =
4. G-a-te =
5. S-a-ve =
6. G-a-ve =
7. M-a-de =
8. N-a-me =
9. C-a-ke =
10. H-a-te =
11. S-a-fe =
12. R-a-ke =
13. t-a-le =
14. w-a-ve =
15. c-a-me =
16. b-a-ke =
17. d-a-te =
18. l-a-ke =
19. p-a-le =
20. l-a-te =
21. m-a-ke =
22. s-a-me =
23. c-a-ve =
24. br-a-ve =
25. sh-a-ve =
26. gr-a-pe =
27. fl-a-me =
28. pl-a-ne =
29. pl-a-te =
30. sn-a-ke =

FORMATION OF SENTENCES WITH SOUND a-e (Sounds as letter 'A')

1. The game is not safe in the plane
2. The gate is made of flame
3. She gave the cake to Ben
4. I use the rake to make the cave
5. He put the grape in the plate for the girl

STEP 25

WORDS WITH SOUND 'ie' (Sounds as letter e)

1. F-ie-ld = Field
2. Th-ie-f =
3. P-ie-ce =
4. Br-ie-f =
5. Gr-ie-f =
6. Ch-ie-f =
7. Sh-ie-ld =
8. Pr-ie-st =
9. Re-lief =
10. Ba-bies

FORMATION OF SENTENCES WITH SOUND 'ie' (Sounds as letter 'e')

1. The babies are in the cots
2. The thief is in the field
3. I baked a piece of cake
4. She is in a brief meeting
5. The drug will relief the pains

STEP 26

WORDS WITH SOUND 'ie' (Sounds as letter 'I')

1. P-ie = Pie
2. T-ie =

3. L-ie =
4. D-ie =
5. Fl-ie-s =
6. Fr-ie-s =
7. Tr-ie-s =
8. Sk-ie-s =
9. Cr-ie-s =
10. Dr-ie-d =
11. Cr-ie-d =
12. Tr-ie-d =
13. Sp-ie-d =

FORMATION OF SENTENCES WITH SOUND 'ie' (Sounds as letter i)

1. I love my pie
2. She wear her tie
3. It is not good to tell lies
4. The flies are on the food
5. He cried to his dad

STEP 27

WORDS ON SOUND 'i-e' sounds as letter i

1. R-i-de = Ride
2. H-i-de =
3. N-i-ne =
4. R-i-pe =
5. L-i-fe =
6. F-i-ve =
7. L-i-ne =
8. P-i-le =
9. M-i-le =
10. P-i-le =
11. T-i-mc =
12. L-i-ke =

13. B-i-ke =
14. W-i-de =
15. M-i-ne =
16. T-i-de =
17. W-i-fe =
18. W-i-ne =
19. Pr-i-ze =
20. Sh-i-ne =
21. Sm-i-le =
22. W-i-pe =
23. Sl-i-de =
24. Wh-i-te =

FORMATION OF SENTENCES WITH SOUND 'i-e'

1. Ese ride the bike to the park
2. I have nine ripe oranges
3. The life i live is in God
4. There are five pipes in the fire
5. The bike is nine and the prize is white

STEP 28
SOUND 'ew'
WORDS WITH SOUND 'ew'

1. F-ew = Few
2. P-ew =
3. N-ew
4. D-ew =
5. Bl-ew =
6. Gr-ew =
7. Dr-ew =
8. Fl-ew =
9. Ch-ew =
10. V-iew =
11. Thr-ew =
12. Sk-ew =

13. St-ew =
14. D-ew =
15. N-ews =

FORMATION OF SENTENCES WITH SOUND 'ew'

1. I have few oranges in my bag
2. I blew my flute in the party
3. The bird flew away in fear
4. I grew up knowing God
5. She threw the cup at me

STEP 29

SOUND 'ue'

WORDS WITH SOUND 'ue'

1. D-ue = Due
2. C-ue =
3. Cl-ue =
4. Gl-ue =
5. Bl-ue =
6. Tr-ue =
7. S-ue =
8. C-u-be =
9. F-u-se =
10. M-ute =
11. Am-use =
12. Fl-ute=

FORMATION OF SENTENCES WITH SOUND 'ue'

1. I have a blue dress
2. There is one cube of sugar in the tea
3. The words she said are true
4. Say the truth and it shall set you free
5. The fuel is in the can

STEP 30

SOUND 'ir'

1. B-ir-d = Bird
2. G-ir-l =
3. D-ir-t =
4. S-ir =
5. F-ir-m =
6. Th-ir-st =
7. F-ir-st =
8. Sh-ir-t =
9. B-ir-th =
10. Th-ir-d =

FORMATION OF SENTENCES WITH SOUND "ir"

1. The bird is in the net
2. There are two girls on the bed
3. Obi threw the dirt in the bin
4. Ann came first in her class
5. Ben has a blue shirt in his room

STEP 31

SOUND 'er'

1. Her = Her
2. Her-b =
3. Her-d =
4. F-er-n =
5. Ne-ver =
6. W-in-ter =
7. Bl-is-ter =
8. Le-tter =
9. Bi-tter =
10. Bu-tter =
11. Li-tter =

12. G-er-m =
13. Mo-ther =
14. Fa-ther =
15. Sis-ter =
16. Bro-ther =
17. Ba-ker =
18. Dan-ger =
19. An-swer =
20. Wea-ther =

FORMATION OF SENTENCES WITH SOUND 'er'

1. I saw a big river in the south
2. He gave me a letter for my mother
3. The butter is sweeter and better
4. The baker baked a tower cake
5. Ben have a father, mother and sisters

STEP 32
SOUND 'or'
WORDS WITH SOUND 'or'

1. Or = Or
2. F-or=
3. P-or-k=
4. T-or-n=
5. H-or-n=
6. W-or-m=
7. C-or-k=
8. F-or-k=
9. L-or-d=
10. C-or-n=
11. M-ore=
12. T-or-ch=
13. St-or-m=
14. N-or-th=
15. Sp-or-t=

16. F-or-ty=
17. P-or-ch=

FORMATION OF SENTENCES WITH SOUND 'or'

1. The cup is for the sport
2. She cannot afford a torn dress
3. There is worm in the corn
4. The lord is with us
5. There are forty short forks in the room

STEP 33:

SOUND 'oi'

WORDS WITH SOUND 'oi'

1. Oi-l= Oil
2. B-oi-l=
3. C-oi-l=
4. C-oi-n=
5. S-oi-l=
6. F-oi-l=
7. N-oi-se=
8. P-oi-nt=
9. Sp-oi-ol=
10. T-oi-let=

FORMATION OF SENTENCES WITH SOUND 'oi'

1. I have a coin
2. We walk on soil
3. She spoil the pen
4. The cake is in the foil
5. She boil the corn in the hut

STEP 34

SOUND 'o-e'

WORDS WITH SOUND 'o-e'

1. B-one= Bone
2. H-ome=
3. R-ope=
4. H-ope=
5. R-ose=
6. N-ose=
7. V-ote=
8. C-oke=
9. J-oke=
10. P-ole=
11. W-oke=
12. C-one=
13. D-oze=
14. Dr-ove=
15. Sm-oke=
16. Sl-ope=
17. Gl-obe=
18. Cl-ose=
19. St-oke=
20. Sp-oke=

FORMATION OF SENTENCES WITH SOUND 'o-e'

1. There is bone in the plate
2. He hanged the rope on the pole
3. Efe went home to cook the food
4. The smoke is in her nose
5. Daddy drove to see the rose

STEP 35

SOUND 'ight'

1. F-ight = Fight
2. R-ight =
3. N-ight =
4. S-ight =
5. Br-ight =
6. T-ight =
7. L-ight =
8. M-ight =
9. Pl-ight =
10. Al-ight =

FORMATION OF SENTENCES WITH SOUND 'ight'

1. As light as a cup
2. He broke his nose in the fight
3. The holly berry is bright red
4. She will faint at the sight of blood
5. Oke wore a tight gown

STEP 36

SOUND 'ng'

1. B-ing = Bing
2. S-ing=
3. W-ing=
4. P-ing=
5. K-ing=
6. Th-ing=
7. R-ing=
8. D-ing=
9. Fly-ing=
10. Pla-ying=

11. Ru-nning=
12. Wri-ting=
13. Jo-gging=
14. Si-tting=
15. Lear-ning=
16. Ea-ting=
17. Jum-ping=
18. En-ding=
19. Buil-ding=

FORMATION OF SENTENCES WITH SOUND 'ing'

1. The bird is flying in the sky
2. Efe is sitting on a chair
3. He has a very good attitude towards learning
4. Ben is jumping on the bed
5. She ring her bell to sing the song

STEP 37

WORDS WITH SOUND 'ong'

1. S-ong = Song
2. G-ong =
3. K-ong =
4. L-ong =
5. Str-ong =
6. Be-long =
7. Sar-ong =
8. Bar-ong =
9. Thr-ong =
10. Wr-ong =

FORMATION OF SENTENCES WITH SOUND 'ong'

1. I love to sing a song
2. I have a long pencil
3. The big pot belong to mummy Ada

4. She shew a strong bone
5. Her answer was wrong

STEP 38

SOUND 'ang'

WORDS WITH SOUND 'ang'

1. H-ang = Hang
2. P-ang =
3. F-ang =
4. G-ang =
5. D-ang =
6. B-ang =
7. R-ang =
8. S-ang =
9. J-ang =
10. L-ang =

FORMATION OF SENTENCES WITH SOUND 'ang'

1. She bang on the door very hard
2. Bola rang the bell for the break
3. I sang a lovely song yesterday
4. Efe hanged her cloth on the rope
5. He moves with bad gang

STEP 39

SOUND 'ank'

1. B-ank = Bank
2. S-ank =
3. R-ank =
4. T-ank =
5. Fr-ank =
6. Pl-ank =
7. Bl-ank =
8. Sl-ank =
9. Ank-le =

10.Sp-ank =

FORMATION OF SENTENCES WITH SOUND 'ank'

1. The bank is close to my store
2. Uncle frank went to the bank
3. His teacher spank him because he made a noise
4. I have a blank paper in my bag
5. Ben has a wide ankle

STEP 40
CONSONANT DIAGRAPHS
SOUND 'cl'

1. Cl-o-ck= Clock
2. Cl-i-ck=
3. Cl-a-p=
4. Cl-a-sh=
5. Cl-ay=
6. Cl-a-n=
7. Cl-a-ss=
8. Cl-i-p=
9. Cl-i-ff=
10. Cl-o-th=
11. Cl-o-p=
12. Cl-o-g=
13. Cl-ing=
14. Cl-ash=
15. Cl-imb=
16. Cl-ou-d=
17. Cl-aw=
18. Cl-u-b=
19. Cl-ow-n=
20. Cl-a-m=

FORMATION OF SENTENCES WITH SOUND ‘cl’

1. She ran to stop the video clip
2. He was the only person to clap
3. The clock is in the class
4. The clay is in the school
5. She climbed the tree to get her cloth

STEP 41
SOUND ‘sl’

1. Sl-a-b= Slab
2. Sl-i-m=
3. Sl-a-p=
4. Sl-i-t=
5. Sl-i-p=
6. Sl-i-ff=
7. SL-I-T=
8. Sl-a-nt=
9. Sl-ee-p=
10. Sl-u-mp=

FORMATION OF SENTENCES WITH SOUND ‘sl’

1. My brother is a slim boy
2. She gave me a slap
3. They slide on the floor
4. Bayo slept today on the couch
5. They slumped in the car

STEP 42

SOUND 'bl'

WORDS WITH SOUND 'bl'

1. Bl-a-b= Blab
2. Bl-o-t=
3. Bl-ow=
4. Bl-e-ss=
5. Bl-i-ss=
6. Bl-a-st=
7. Bl-ee-d=
8. Bl-ink=
9. Bl-ew=
10. Bl-ame=

FORMATION OF SENTENCES WITH SOUND 'bl'

1. The book is blank
2. He blasted the exam
3. I am bless
4. The girl blew the sand into his eyes
5. The boy was blamed for opening the gate

STEP 43

SOUND 'fl'

WORDS WITH SOUND 'fl'

1. Fl-a-g= Flag
2. Fl-a-t=
3. Fl-o-p=
4. Fl-a-b=
5. Fl-i-t=
6. Fl-i-p=
7. Fl-ame=
8. Fl-are
9. Fl-ow=

10.Fl-ee=

FORMATION OF SENTENCES WITH SOUND 'fl'

1. The flag is green in colour
2. The bed is too flat
3. The flab is very small
4. The flame of fire is very hot
5. The flit is in the house

STEP 44
SOUND 'gl'
WORDS WITH SOUND 'gl'

1. Gl-a-d= Glad
2. Gl-ow=
3. Gl-ue=
4. Gl-a-ss=
5. Gl-are=
6. Gl-ea-m=
7. Gl-ide=
8. Gl-obe=
9. Gl-ove=
10. Gl-ory=

FORMATION OF SENTENCES WITH SOUND 'gl'

1. The snake glided across the road
2. The sun glow in the day time
3. There are some broken glasses on the floor
4. The glory of God is upon my life
5. I am glad to be alive

STEP 45

SOUND ‘pl’

WORDS WITH SOUND ‘pl’

1. Pl-ay= Play
2. Pl-ea=
3. Pl-an=
4. Pl-ai-n=
5. Pl-ace=
6. Pl-ea-se=
7. Pl-o-t=
8. Pl-u-ck=
9. Pl-u-mp
10. Pl-ea-d

FORMATION OF SENTENCES WITH SOUND ‘pl’

1. Ben play in the field everyday
2. Ann has plans for the weekend
3. She hit the ball with the big plank
4. My dad is planting a flower
5. They plot to kill the king

STEP 46

SOUND ‘br’

WORDS WITH SOUND ‘br’

1. Br-a-g= Brag
2. Br-aces=
3. Br-ai-n=
4. Br-ake=
5. Br-and=
6. Br-ass=
7. Br-ave=
8. Br-ea-d=
9. Br-ea-k=
10. Br-ea-th=

11. Br-ea-st=
12. Br-ee-d=
13. Br-ee-ze=
14. Br-ibe=
15. Br-ew=
16. Br-ide=
17. Br-idge=
18. Br-ief=
19. Br-im=
20. Br-ing

FORMATION OF SENTENCES WITH SOUND 'br'

1. That house is build on bricks
2. The bride is white as snow
3. The bridge is on the road
4. Temi have a brand new belt
5. They held a brief meeting in the class

STEP 47
SOUND'cr'
WORDS WITH SOUND 'cr'

1. Cr-a-b= Crab
2. Cr-a-ck=
3. Cr-a-ft=
4. Cr-a-sh
5. Cr-ane=
6. Cr-awl=
7. Cr-ea-m=
8. Cr-ea-k=
9. Cr-ea-k=
10. Cr-ee-p=
11. Cr-e-st=
12. Cr-ew=
13. Cr-i-sp=

14. Cr-oa-k=
15. Cr-o-p=
16. Cr-o-ss=
17. Cr-ow-d=
18. Cr-ow-d=
19. Cr-ow-n=
20. Cr-uel=
21. Cr-ush=

FORMATION OF SENTENCES WITH SOUND 'cr'

1. The crew had crisis in the crane
2. The cream is very nice
3. The crops are very green
4. The crowd are in the park
5. I have a pink crown

STEP 48

SOUND 'dr'

WORDS WITH SOUND 'dr'

1. Dr-i-ll= Drill
2. Dr-aw=
3. Dr-ai-n=
4. Dr-a-ft=
5. Dr-a-g=
6. Dr-a-ma=
7. Dr-a-nk=
8. Dr-ea-m=
9. Dr-e-ss=
10. Dr-ew=
11. Dr-ied=
12. Dr-i-ft=
13. Dr-i-ll=
14. Dr-i-nk=

15. Dr-i-p=
16. Dr-i-ve=
17. Dr-o-p==
18. Dr-oo-p=
19. Dr-u-m=
20. Dr-u-nk=

FORMATION OF SENTENCES WITH SOUND 'dr'

1. Sam drew the man that drank to drunk
2. The river is dry at this time of the year
3. Ben left his car for Ann to drive
4. She tore the dress and drop on the floor
5. I have drafted a letter to the bank

STEP 49
SOUND 'fr'
WORDS WITH SOUNDS 'fr'

1. Fr-y= Fry
2. Fr-ai-l=
3. Fr-ee=
4. Fr-ame=
5. Fr-aud=
6. Fr-ee-ze=
7. Fr-e-sh=
8. Fr-ie-d=
9. Fr-iend=
10. Fr-ight=
11. Fr-inge=
12. Fr-i-ck=
13. Fr-og=
14. Fr-o-m=
15. Fr-o-nt=
16. Fr-o-st=
17. Fr-ow-n=
18. Fr-ui-t=

19. Fr-oze=
20. Fr-o-zen=

FORMATION OF SENTENCES WITH SOUND 'fr'

1. Let the bird go free
2. The frogs are in the frame
3. Ben bought some fresh oranges
4. I fried the rice on Friday
5. Ann bought a dozen of frozen fruits

STEP 50
SOUND 'gr'
WORDS WITH SOUND 'gr'

1. Gr-a-b= Grab
2. Gr-ai-n=
3. Gr-ace=
4. Gr-ade=
5. Gr-a-m=
6. Gr-a-nd=
7. Gr-a-nny=
8. Gr-a-nt=
9. Gr-ape=
10. Gr-a-sp=
11. Gr-a-ph=
12. Gr-a-ss=
13. Gr-ave=
14. Gr-eat=
15. Gr-eet=
16. Gr-a-vel=
17. Gr-a-vy=
18. Gr-aze=
19. Gr-een=
20. Gr-ee-d=

FORMATION OF SENTENCES WITH SOUNDS 'gr'

1. The grain is too small
2. I had a great day
3. Favour greet her mum every morning
4. The grape is green in colour
5. Her grand mother granted her request

STEP 51
SOUND 'pr'
WORDS WITH SOUND 'pr'

1. Pr-ay= Pray
2. Pr-ide=
3. Pr-oud=
4. pr-ea-ch=
5. pr-e-ss=
6. pr-e-tty=
7. pr-ey=
8. pr-ice=
9. pr-iest=
10. pr-ime=
11. pr-ince=
12. pr-i-son=
13. pr-ize=
14. pr-o-fit=
15. pr-oo-f=
16. pr-o-duct=
17. pr-o-gr-am=
18. pro-ject=
19. pr-ove=

FORMATION OF SENTENCES WITH SOUND 'pr'

1. The price of ball is very high
2. The priest prayed for the progress of the project
3. The pretty girl was proved to be the prime suspect
4. The boy is in the prison
5. The product is of a high value

STEP 52

SOUND ‘sm’

WORDS WITH SOUND ‘sm’

1. Sm-a-ck= Smack
2. Sm-all=
3. Sm-ar-t=
4. Sm-a-sh=
5. Sm-ell=
6. Sm-ile=
7. Sm-oke=
8. Sm-oo-th=
9. Sm-ear=
10. Sm-o-ky=

FORMATION OF SENTENCES WITH SOUND ‘sm’

1. There is a smoky hut in my street
2. There is a bad smell in the room
3. Mrs. Tega had a big smile on her face
4. Runo always look smart
5. Mr. Ade have a small farm

STEP 53

SOUND ‘sn’

WORDS WITH SOUND ‘sn’

1. Sn-a-ck= Snack
2. Sn-ore=
3. Sn-a-p=
4. Sn-ai-l=
5. Sn-ake=
6. Sn-ow=
7. Sn-iff=
8. Sn-atch=
9. Sn-eak=

10.Sn-eeze=

FORMATION OF SENTENCES WITH SOUND 'sn'

1. The pet sneaked out of the room
2. The snake is very long
3. The small snail crawl very slow
4. The dog sniffed the bag of fish
5. Ken snapped out of his deep sleep

STEP 54
SOUND 'sp'
WORDS WITH SOUND 'sp'

1. Sp-ace= Space
2. Sp-ade=
3. Sp-ank=
4. Sp-are=
5. Sp-ar-k=
6. Sp-i-t=
7. Sp-ea-k=
8. Sp-ear=
9. sp-e-ll=
10. sp-el-t=
11. sp-e-nd=
12. sp-ice=
13. sp-ied=
14. sp-ill=
15. sp-in=
16. sp-ine=
17. sp-it=
18. sp-at=
19. sp-oi-l=
20. sp-oke=

FORMATION OF SENTENCES WITH SOUND 'sp'

1. The space in the lab is too small
2. The girl spilled the wine on the floor
3. Ben spilled water on the box
4. The teacher spoke to Anne in the classroom
5. The baby spat the bread on her mum

STEP 55
SOUND 'st'
WORDS WITH SOUND 'st'

1. St-a-b= Stab
2. St-a-ck=
3. St-a-ff=
4. St-age=
5. St-ia-n=
6. St-air=
7. St-ick=
8. St-ill=
9. St-a-mp=
10. St-a-nd=
11. St-art=
12. St-ar=
13. St-ar-ch=
14. St-arve=
15. St-ate=
16. St-ay=
17. St-e-p=
18. St-ea-m=
19. St-ea-l=
20. St-e-m=

FORMATION OF SENTENCES WITH SOUND 'st'

1. The boy stab the goat in the belly
2. The staffs are meeting in the stair case
3. The star is in the sky

4. Ben threw the sticks into the fire
5. The stage in the state is full of stars

STEP 56
SOUND 'sw'
WORDS WITH SOUND 'sw'

1. Sw-a-b= Swab
2. Sw-ee-p=
3. Sw-i-ng=
4. Sw-i-m=
5. Sw-ipe=
6. Sw-itch=
7. Sw-an=
8. Sw-oo-p=
9. Sw-ar-m=
10. Sw-ee-t=

FORMATION OF SENTENCES WITH SOUND 'sw'

1. Kemi loves to sweep in the morning
2. Ada swims in the pool everyday
3. The sweet is in my bag
4. Switch on the light in the room
5. I have a swing in my school

STEP 57
SOUND "sk"

1. Sk – y = Sky
2. Sk – i – p =
3. Sk – u – ll =
4. Sk – i – ll =
5. Sk – ate =
6. Sk – e – le – ton =
7. Sk - etch =
8. Sk – id =

9. Sk – in =

10. Sk – ift =

SENTENCES WITH SOUND "sk"

1. I admired her skill at driving
2. The car skidded on a pool of oil
3. The sky is very far
4. Her skin was full of rashes
5. She wore a pink skirt to the party

STEP 58
SOUND "sc"

1. Sc-an= Scan
2. Sc-rew=
3. Sc-ore=
4. Sc-rub=
5. Sc-roll=
6. Sc-ream=
7. Sc-reech=
8. Sc-reen=
9. Sc-ratch=
10. Sc-rape=

SENTENCES WITH SOUNDS "sc"

1. Obi is learning how to read and write in school
2. Mary's scalp is very dark
3. She screamed when she saw the snake
4. The screen is very wide
5. He scrolled his phone to check the date
6. Bola scraped the mud off her shoe

STEP 59
SOUND "tw"

1. Tw-in= Twin
2. Tw-ist=
3. Tw-itch=

4. Tw-ice=
5. Tw-enty=
6. Tw-ee-zers=
7. Tw-el-fth=
8. Tw-in-kle=
9. Twi-tter
10. Tw – en – tieth =
11. Tw – ain=

SENTENCES WITH SOUND " TW "

1. The twin's names are John and Joan
2. She has twenty pieces of silver spoon
3. She plaited a twisted hair
4. Daniel prayed twice a day
5. She came home on the twelfth hour

STEP 60

SYLLABLES

In this section we will learn how to pronounce longer words with the use of syllables?

What is Syllable?

Syllable is the breaking down of words into smaller units. There are three major types of Syllables they are:

1. Mono – syllables (one syllables)
2. Di – syllable (two syllables)
3. Multi – Syllable (More than three syllables)

Examples of Syllables with words

Mono – Syllables	Di – Syllables	Multi - Syllables
1	ta – ble	de – co – ra – tion
Fat	Bas – ket	De – fi – ceien – cy
Start	Man – go	In – for – ma – tion
Stop	Cul – ture	Cul – ti – va – tion
Men	De – feat	In – for – ma – tion
We	Tea – cher	Cal – cu – la – tor

STEP 61

In this section, we will break down words into syllables. My objective is for the learners to be able to pronounce longer words with many letters.

STEP 62
SYLLABLES

1. A – ban – don = Abandon
2. A – bbre – via – tion =
3. Ab – do – men =
4. A – bi – li – ty =
5. A – bo – lish =
6. A – board =
7. Ab – scess =
8. Ab – sence =
9. Ab – so – lutely =
10. Ab – sor – bent =
11. A – ca – de – my =
12. A – cce – le – ra – tor =
13. A – ccep – ta – ble =
14. A – cci – den – ta – lly =
15. A – ccom – pa – ny =
16. A-ccom - mo - da – tion =
17. A – ccom – plish =
18. A – ccor – ding =
19. A – chieve – ment =
20. A – ccu – sa – tion =
21. A – ccu – stomed =
22. Ac – know – ledge =
23. Ac – quain – tance =
24. Ad – just – able =
25. Ad – mi – ni – stra – tion =
26. Ad – mi – ssion =
27. Ad – ven – tu – rous =

28. Ad – ver – tise – ment =
29. Aero – plane =
30. A – ffec – tion – ate – ly =
31. Earth – quake =
32. Earth – worm =
33. E – co - no – mi – cal =
34. E – du – ca – tion =
35. E – ffi – cient – ly =
36. E – lec – tri – cian =
37. E – le – men – tary =
38. E – le – phan – tia – sis =
39. Em – bar – rass – ment =
40. Em – broi – dery =
41. E – mer – gen – cy =
42. E – mi – gra – tion =
43. E – mo – tion – al =
44. Em – pha – si – zing =
45. Em – ploy – ment =
46. En – cou – rage – ment =
47. En – cy - clo – pae – dia =
48. E – ner – ge – tic =
49. En – gage – ment =
50. En – gi – nee – ring =
51. En – joy – ment =
52. En – ter – tain – ment =
53. En – thu – sia – sm =
54. En – ve – lope =
55. En – vi – ron – ment =
56. E – pi – de – mic =
57. E – qua – li – ty =
58. E – qua – tor =
59. E – quip – ment =
60. E – qui – va – lent =
61. Ex – cute – ment =
62. Ex – clu – ding =
63. I – den – ti – fi – ca – tion =
64. I – lle – gi – ti – mate =

65. I – lli – terate =
66. I – llu – stra – tion =
67. I – ma – gi – na – ry =
68. I – mi – ta – tion =
69. I – mma – ture =
70. I – mme – diate – ly =
71. I – mmen – sely =
72. I – mmi – grant =
73. I – mmu – ni – za – tion =
74. Im – pa – tient =
75. Im – per – ti – nent =
76. Im – por – tance =
77. Im – po – ssi – ble =
78. Im – pre – ssion =
79. Im – pre – ssive =
80. Im – prove – ment
81. Ina – bi – lity =
82. In – accu – rate =
83. Inci – den – tally =
84. In – clu – ding =
85. In – com - plete =
86. Incon – ve – nient =
87. In – crea – sing – ly =
88. In - cre – di – ble =
89. In – cu – ra – ble =
90. Inde – pen – dence =
91. In – di – ge – nous =
92. In – di – vi – dual
93. Obli – ga – tion =
94. Ob – ser – va – tion =
95. Ob – struc – tion =
96. Occu – pa – tion =
97. O – cca –sio – na – lly =
98. Occu – pa – tion
99. Oc –to – ber =
100. O – ffi – cial =
101. O – lym – pic =

102. Ope – ra – tion =
103. O – pi – nion =
104. O – ppo – nent =
105. O – ppor – tu – ni – ty
106. Op – ti – cian =
107. Opti – mi – stic =
108. Or – ga – ni – za – tion =
109. Un – be – lie – va – ble =
110. Un – cer – tian =
111. Un – com – for – ta – ble =
112. Un – co – mmon =
113. Un – con – sious
114. Un – coun – ta – ble =
115. Un – der – gra – duate =
116. Un – der – line =
117. Un – der – neath =
118. Un – pel – sant =
119. Un – po – pu - lar =
120. Un – rea – so – na – ble =
121. Un – re – lia – ble =
122. Un – sa – tis – fac – tory =
123. Un – sel – fish =
124. Un – stea – dy =
125. Un – ti – dy =
126. Un – true =
127. Un – sui – ta – ble =
128. Un – sym – pa – the – tic
129. Un – usua – lly =
130. Un – wi – lling - ly =
131. Un – wra – pping =
132. Up – to – date =

STEP 63

Note: *There are some sounds that produces words with different spellings but has the same sound, we will be listing out the sounds with words so you don't get confused when you see some words with the same sound and different spellings. For further explanation we will be using the monophthong and diphthong sounds, which will also include the use of phonetic symbols, for further information about the phonetic symbol check the dictionary.*

What is Monophthong

A Monophthong is a single vowel sound.

The 12 Monophthong Sounds, Symbols and Words

1. /i:/ spelt as: 'e' 'ee' 'ea' 'ie' 'I' 'e'– seat, beeds, feet, bee, feed, seize, jean, police, people, key
2. /I/ 'i' 'y' e,a – fit, sit, lady, pretty, kick, lick, bin, dip, kid, jig
3. /e/ 'e' 'ay' – says, red, head, spread, dead, dead, bread, step, fetch, ten
4. /□/ 'a' – pan, flat, cat, pat, match, sam, pack, chat, had, gas.
5. /a:/ 'ar' 'a' 'au' – mark, chart, part, hard, heart, dart, psalm, laugh
6. /ʊ/ 'u' 'ou' 'oo' – pull, put, full, bush, look, good, foot, shook, crook, sugar
7. /u:/ spelt as: 'u' 'oo' 'ui' – fool, blue, cool, tool, food, rude, use, June, tune, moon.
8. /o/ spelt as 'o' 'a' – what, want, wash, quality, soft, cob, dot, from, hot, mop
9. /ʌ/ 'u' 'o' 'oo' 'ou' – young, blood, flood, some, above, love, son, shut, come sun, cut, sum, gum
10. /ɜ:/ 'ir' 'er' 'ur' – bird, burn, girl, burst, burn, wood, heard, dirty, birth, shirt
11. /ɔ:/ spelt as: 'o' 'a' 'oor' 'our' 'aw' 'al' – Horse, cord, floor, talk, chalk, tall, saw, warn, warm, sport
12. /ə/ spelt as: 'or' 'er' 'a' – Amount, among, ago, agree, mentor, miracle, teacher, method, father

DIPHTHONG

WHAT IS DIPHTHONG?

Diphthong is a sound formed by the combination of two vowels in a single syllable.

EXAMPLES OF DIPHTHONG SOUNDS AND WORDS

1. /ei/ spelt as : a-e, ay, ai ➡ bake cake, make, say, again e.t.c
2. /ai/ spelt as : y, igh, i-e ➡ try, by, fight, pile. e.t.c
3. /əʊ/ spelt as : oa, ow, ol ➡ coat, goat, slow, hole e.t.c
4. / əʊ/ spelt as : ow, ou, ➡ town, down, house, shout, e.t.c
5. /ɔi/ spelt as : oi, oy ➡ oil, toy, boil, coil, e.t.c
6. /eə/ spelt as air, a-e ➡ air, hair, share, e.t.c

SUMMARY OF SOME GRAMMATICAL TERMS

VOWELS AND CONSONANTS

1. There are five vowels in the alphabet

   These are A E I O U

   a e i o u

2. There are twenty-one consonants in the alphabet

   These are B C D F G H J K L M

   b c d f g h j k l m

   N P Q R S T V W X Y

   N p q r s t v w x y

   Z

   z

Note: The English alphabets are made up of twenty-six letters

NOUNS

What is a noun?

A noun is a name of a person, animal, place or things

Person	animal	places	things
Mr Issa	goat	Delta	pen
Obi	dog	market	pencil
Esther	lion	church	ruler
Eriga	elephant	Edo	table
David	cow	Abia	chair

PROPER NOUN

Proper nouns are special names of person, pets, days of the week and months of the year

Examples

Person	pets	days	months
Favour	snoopy	Tuesday	March
Daniel	bingo	Wednesday	August
Tama	Jackie	Thursday	September
Thehila	spunky	Friday	November
Excel	tommy	Sunday	February

NOTE: Always use capital letter to begin a proper noun

Examples: I gave the pen to <u>D</u>aniel

He came on <u>M</u>onday. E.t.c

COMMON NOUN

A common noun is a name commonly given to a noun.

Examples: school, farmer, village, girl, boy. E.t.c

Note: do not use capital letter to write a common noun except it is written at the beginning of a sentence

Examples:

1. The <u>girl</u> is in the room
2. <u>Girls</u> are in the room

SINGULAR AND PLURAL

Singular means one. Plural refers to more than one

TAKE NOTE OF THE FOLLOWING

1. Some nouns add only(s) to make plurals

   Examples:

Singular	plural
1. Ruler	rulers
2. Bag	bags

2. Some add 'es'

   Examples:

Singular	plural
Box	boxes
Class	classes

3. Some changes 'y' into 'ies'

   Examples: baby-babies, city-cities
4. Some changes 'fe' OR 'f' to 'ves'

   Examples: calf- calves, wife-wives
5. Some changes their vowels or middle letters to make their plurals

   Examples: woman-women, man-men
6. While others add "en" or "ren" to make plurals

   Examples: ox-oxen, child-children

GENDER

Gender refers to he or she, male or female, masculine or feminine.

Examples: brother- sister, prince-princess

POSSESSIONS

Possession means showing ownership

Examples

Long form: the dress which belong to the woman

Short form: the woman's dress

COUNTABLE AND UNCOUNTABLE NOUN

1. Countable nouns are things we can count
2. Uncountable noun are things we can't count

Note: we use a, some few, afew for countable nouns	we use some or a little for uncountable nouns
Examples: a chair	some air
a table	some water
a ruler	a little salt
some books	a little sand
a few plates	

ARTICLES

Article is the use of a, an, and the

1. a is use for nouns that begin with a consonant
2. an is use for nouns that begins with a vowel (a,e,i,o,u)
3. The is use for noun you know about already

Example: A dog, an apple, the man

PRONOUN

Pronoun are used in place of nouns

Examples of pronoun: I, you, me, he, him, her, us, them, they, it, she e.t.c

Noun: The dress is for Ada

Pronoun: it is for her

TAKE NOTE

In relative pronouns

Who: is used for person

Which: is used for animals and things

In demonstrative pronoun

This and that are use for singular

Those and these are use for plural

ADJECTIVES

Adjectives are words that describe nouns

Examples of adjective are: clean, long, low, old, new, small, big, beautiful, sweet

Examples: I have a beautiful dress

VERB

A verb is an action word

Examples: I write, I sleep, I run, I jump

PRESENT TENSE AND PAST TENSE

1. Present tense means action that happen now
2. Past tense means action that happened in the past

   NOTE THE FOLLOWING

1. Sometimes you need to add 'ed' to some verb to make them past tense
   Example: work- worked
   Clap-clapped
2. Some change vowel to make past tense
   Examples: fall-fell
   Come -came
3. Others make their past tense differently
   Examples: go-went, is-was

Adverb: adverb are words that tells us more about a verb, most times adverbs ends with –ly

Examples: happy-happily
Sad- sadly

CONTRACTIONS

Contraction means to make a word shorter by using the apostrophe (')

Examples:	did not	-	did'nt
	Has not	-	hasn't

ANTONYMS

Antonyms are words that are opposite in meaning

Examples: right- wrong, long-short

SYNONYMS:

Synonyms are words that mean the same as the other.

Examples: rich- wealthy, correct- right

SIMILES

Smiles means things that are alike.

Examples:

1. As wise as Solomon
2. As sweet as honey

SPELLING DRILL

THINGS IN AND AROUND THE HOME

1. Bucket
2. Basket
3. Cutlass
4. Television
5. Gas cylinder
6. Bed
7. Toothbrush
8. Refrigerator
9. Store
10. Kettle

THINGS IN THE SCHOOL

1. Table
2. Chair
3. Bag
4. Chalk
5. Waste bin
6. Swing
7. Black board
8. White board
9. Bell
10. Desk

THINGS IN THE MARKET

1. Pepper
2. Fish
3. Yam
4. Water bottle
5. Orange
6. Milk
7. Milo
8. Vegetable
9. Meat
10. Garri

TYPES OF FOOD

1. Rice
2. Beans
3. Plantain
4. Soap
5. Onion
6. Cocoyam
7. Potatoe
8. Garri
9. Water yam
10. Yam

DAYS OF THE WEEK

Sunday

Monday

Tuesday

Wednesday

Thursday

Friday

Saturday

MONTHS OF THE YEAR

January

February

March

April

May

June

July

August

September

October

November

December

READING PRACTICE

In this last section, the objective is to test the reading ability of the learner or reader after he or she has gone through the different steps in this book, and also to impact or create some moral values into the mind of the learner or reader.

Secondly, this last section also contains a topic on financial management, aim at drilling the learners with some complex words. Some of the words will be selected out and splits into syllables for better understanding of the leaner or reader.

DILIGENCE

Diligent is having or showing care and conscientiousness in one's work or duties Example: "after diligent searching, he found the parcel"

Another name for diligent are INDUSTRIOUS OR INCREDULOUS, HARD-WORKING, ASSIDUOUS, CONSIENTIOUS, PUNCTILIOUS, METICULOUS, PAINSTAKING, TANACIOUS, RIGOROUS, SEDULOUS PERTINACIOUS, ZEALOUS, COMMITTED, INDEFATIGABLE, LABORIOUS, SLOGGING, PLODDING, DEDICATED, TIRELESS ETC.

The definition of diligent is hard working and done with painstaking effort. Someone who is diligent, works hard in a careful and thorough way. Diligent comes from the Latin word "diligere" which means "to value highly, take delight in", but in English it has always meant careful and hard – working.

In this way, diligence may rather be regarded as a combination of both hard work and patience. It is also one of the most important attributes of a person. If you are a student, you can make yourself successful in your studies on the basis of your diligence. May God help us all.

SOME COMPLEX WORDS IN THE TOPIC "DELIGENT"

E-co-no-mi-cal

Con-scien-tious-ness

Sear-ching

Par-cel

In-dus-trious

In-cre-du-lous

A-ssi-duous	Con-scien-tious
Punc-ti-lious	Me-ti-cu-lous
Pain-sta-king	Te-na-cious
Ri-go-rous	Se-du-lous
Per-ti-na-cious	Zea-lous
Co-mmi-tted	In-de-fati-ga-ble
La-bo-rious	Slo-gging
Plo-dding	De-di-ca-ted
Tire-less	Di-li-gere
Pa-tience	Per-sis-tent

HONESTY

Honesty is the quality of being truthful or in a simple form, honesty means saying the truth at all time. Honesty helps in developing good attributes like KINDNESS, DISCIPLINE, TRUTHFULNESS, MORAL INTEGRITY and more. Lying, cheating, lack of trust, steal, greed and immoral attribute have no part in honesty. Honest people are sincere, trustworthy and loyal, throughout their life. Honesty or truthfulness is a facet of moral character that connotes positive and virtuous attributes such as integrity, truthfulness, including straight forwardness of conduct, along with the absence of lying, cheating, theft, etc. honesty also involves being trustworthy, loyal, fair and sincere.

COMPLEX WORDS IN THE TOPIC "HONESTY"

Kind-ness	Di-sci-pline
Truth-ful-ness	In-te-gri-ty
I-mmo-ral	Sin-cere
Trus-wor-thy	Lo-yal
Vir-tuous	A-ttri-butes
For-ward-ness	Sin-cere

OBEDIENCE

Obedient is complying or willing to comply with an order or request; submissive to another's authority. Another word for obedience are complaint, law abiding, deferential, amenable, tractable, acquiescent, dutiful, respectful, duteous, disciplined, observant, manageable, conformable, docile, biddable, submissive, tame, meek, passive, unresisting, yielding, subservient, servile etc

NOTE: the opposite of obedience is DISOBEDIENT, REBELLIOUS, AND UNRULY etc. Obedience therefore in human behavior, is a form of "social influence in which a person yields to explicit instructions or orders from an authority figure". Obedience is generally distinguished from compliance, which is behavior influenced by peers, and from conformity which is behavior intended to match that of the majority. For example: students are expected to be quiet and obedient in the classroom.

SOME COMPLEX WORDS IN THE TOPIC "OBEDIENCE"

Sub-mi-ssive	Au-tho-ri-ty
Com-plaint	De-feren-tial
A-me-na-ble	Trac-ta-ble
Ac-quie-scent	Du-teous
Res-pect-ful	Di-sci-plined
Ob-ser-vant	Ma-na-gea-ble
Con-for-ma-ble	Do-cile
Bi-dda-ble	Sub-mi-ssive
Pa-ssive	Un-re-sis-ting
Yiel-ding	Sub-se-vient
Ser-vile	Re-be-llious

Un-ruly — Dis-tin-guished

Com-pliance — In-fluenced

Con-for-mi-ty

VALUE YOUR WORK

Man was created to impact his world through his work. Every man that desires to command a shining destiny must be passionate and diligent worker. Give yourself to work and you will end as a shining star in destiny. Work is blessing to man, not a curse. God is a hard worker and He made man in His own image. It is an abomination for any man to be idle, lazy and jobless. There are no stagnant or idle stars in Gods universe. No idle person will shine in life. Your promotion and profit in life is tied to your work ethic and attitude. It is your work that determines your worth.

Take note of the following truths about work:

1. **Value and celebrate work and labour:** It is our God-given key for potential development and expression. Never frown at work.
2. **At every point in time, have a particular work you are engaging yourself in:** Never have a season of joblessness. Give yourself to either an education, apprenticeship, occupation, or self-employment. There is always something to do; find it and give yourself to it.
3. **Take prompt action on every idea or dream you have**: Every genuine vision and inspiration should produce action and motion. Make up your mind on issues quickly. Take decisions promptly and act on them speedily. Men of high impact always act on ideas promptly
4. **Avoid time wasters and time wasting:** Do not waste your own time and do not let others waste it for you. Postponement and procrastination steal time and waste destiny. Anything worth doing is worth being done on time. Do

not waste time in endless, aimless analysis and consideration. Think and think fast. Consider all your possible options quickly

There is never a perfect time for doing anything. Learn to make the best use of the time you have.

SOME COMPLEX WORDS IN THE TOPIC "VALUE YOUR WORK"

Pa-ssio-nate	Di-li-gent
A-bo-mi-na-tion	Stag-nant
Uni-verse	De-ve-lop-ment
Ex-pre-ssion	Fr-own
Job-less-ness	A-ppren-tice-ship
O-ccu-pa-tion	Ge-nuine
Post-pone-ment	Pro-cra-sti-na-tion
Con-si-dera-tion	Aim-less
Ana-ly-sis	In-spi-ra-tion

AN ECONOMY TERM: FINANCIAL GLOBALIZATION

Globalization is the integration of national economies through trade, capital flows and the accompanying convergence of economic policies. In the field of creativity and culture, globalization has become a well known word over the years, but globalization has become a household word literally since early 1990s when financial globalization kicked off. During the period, the trade obstructions between nations were broken apart, and the flow of capital and corporate investments between deferent countries were embarked upon.

One of the many definitions of financial globalization integration of domestic financial system of a country with the global financial markets and institutions.

Financial globalization is also defined as an amalgamation of domestic financial system of a particular country with the international organizations as well as financial market. Enabling framework of financial globalization essentially includes liberalization and deregulation of the domestic financial sector as well as liberalization of the capital account. As economics progressively integrate globally, Pari Passu the financial structures of markets and world of finance charge. Massive growth have been noticed in global economy in the last couple of years, and in the field of technology, more precisely in transport and communication there was a silent revolution which made the globalization an obvious choice.

SOME COMPLEX WORDS IN THE TOPIC "FINANCIAL GLOBALIZATION"

Glo-ba-li-za-tion	Na-tio-nal
Con-ver-gence	Cre-a-ti-vi-ty
Cor-porate	In-vest-ment
Em-barked	In-ter-gra-tion
In-sti-tu-tion	In-ter-na-tio-nal
Li-bera-li-za-tion	Re-vo-lu-tion
Pro-gre-ssive-ly	Pre-aset-ly
Des-ta-bi-li-zing	

www.ingramcontent.com/pod-product-compliance
Lightning Source LLC
LaVergne TN
LVHW052053160826
845678LV00015B/3200